DEDICATED

TO

ANDREW DAVID SWIFT

WE RAISE OUR GLASSES TO LIFE!

Cover and artwork 'Turmoil': Martina Swift

CONTENTS

- What makes you happy? ………Page 6
- In honour of you……………Page 12
- The Sun cherishes Her Sunflower…Page 14
- The Sun and His bride….Page 15
- Sunflower reflects Sun….Page 16
- Sunflower: The proverbial woman..Page 18
- My two joys……………..Page 19
- To 3 year old Hattie……..Page 20
- India……………Page 22
- Say hello to tomorrow……………Page 23
- As time goes by……………Page 24
- For just one minute…..Page 25
- Home…………Page 27
- The Journey Motif; River Mimram ……Page 28
- Come let us ponder together…Page 29

- Soon, I will lose all three dear brothers ……Page 31
- Coronavirus……………Page 35
- Frontline daughter……………Page 38
- Baby……………Page 39
- Strange sighting on a Turkish beach ………Page 40
- Goodbye-ing Turk……………Page 41
- I have lost my dog and my father ……………Page 45
- The gap in my heart ……………Page 46
- What about me?…………Page 47
- Dear dad……………Page 49
- Dear mum is scared to stay with me ………Page 50
- The cost of food, baby sister ……………Page 51

- Someone I should know well ....Page 54
- Trans: life adrift................Page 55
- You, Me or Us......Page 56
- The value of woman ....Page 57
- Pest control...............Page 58
- My son...............Page 59
- Shackles...............Page 60
- The cusp of death................Page 61

LIFE AND LOVE

~o~

What makes you happy?

The fullness of clusters of blossoms as a crown of bush, on a tree.

The flutter of white and pink blossoms in the gentle spring wind.

Jack, Jill, and leverets dash about, then scurry into plants and bushes.

The dancing blue eyes of my lover.

The freedom of soft scraggly beginnings of a beard on its first outings during quarantine.

The carefree laughter of children chasing elusive bubbles.

A treelined path with branches on either side, curved into an arch, offering shade from a warm walk.

A bed of bluebells on a hill, sheltered in the cradle of a woodland.

The hue of bluebells in a field caught in a ray of sunlight.

Cycling in summer, the warmth of the evening breeze zipping downhill at 20 miles per hour on a man-made death trap.

A walk after the rain, as the sun soaks up the moisture, a gulp cleanses the cobwebs of my many screens.

Light teasing its way through the leaves and branches on a quiet evening.

Orange, yellow, and dusky white skies as the sun settles down for the night.

Frank Sinatra's crooning, Jacques Brel wailing 'Ne me quitte pas' and Edith Piaf who regrets nothing.

The many greens of my daily walk. Leaves of many colours, all green: the olive-green leaves, lime greens, conference pear greens, cactus greens, golden delicious greens, cucumber greens, pistachio greens, mint greens, avocado greens, asparagus greens, sea greens – green like the hue of shallow seawater as seen from the surface. Green silver brown and grey trees. Green yellow and rust grass. Green brown and black birds. Green, brown and white spotted butterflies.

To see passion, dance in the blue eyes of a lover for his garden.

When a Goldfinch perches on a branch and waits patiently as I fumble with my camera, then I capture a piece of nature's art at its finest.

The choir of skylarks playing hide and seek in long spring grass.

The patter of rain on the roof whilst I am wrapped up cosy and warm under my duvet.

The rhythmic beating of African drums.

The crisscross feverish rhythm of intoxicating Cuban beats.

The affirming smiley face of a speed indicator '20 miles per hour', whooshing downhill on my bicycle, the sweet gush of air on my face and the loud wind as I cut through it.

The physicality of moving through space, the joy of exerting my body, the pump of adrenaline soaring through my body and the rush of dopamine gushing, lifting me to a high plane.

Mellifluous arrangement of a captivating poem.

I like to wade into a pool of cool water, slide slowly into its indulgent smooth essence.

Water lapping all about my frame, flows freely over my body, toes, ears, eyes, and nose. It envelopes me. I like to glide languidly through the length of a pool. My right-hand cupping a handful lazily moves me forward on to the next stroke.

My left hand then takes its turn cupping some water, my head tilted to one side to capture a gulp of air and then face down into the water.

I savour each moment.

Later, I melt into the warm watery blanket, boneless, completely immersed in liquid gold, each cell feeding on the hedonism of the moment, in utter silence, eyes closed, always with my eyes closed. – Immersed in silence.

The limits of a terrestrial anatomy then demand I rise to the surface and continue my reverie afloat, like an otter, in a happy buoyant state, somewhat envious of all amphibians on planet earth.

I love it best when the pool is all mine

I can roll, swirl and spiral like a coil the length of the pool in glorious abandon.

I climb out of the pool, water runs off my skin smoothly, flows freely down my body. I look back longingly at the tantalizing mass of decadence, the distance between us traced by tell-tale wet footprints.

I tear myself away, yearning for the next rendezvous.

Happiness!

In honour of You

Each day
I will smile with my eyes
I will be grateful, in honour of You.

Each day
I will look a little closer at a petal
I will be grateful, in honour of You.

Each day
I will skip at least once
I will be grateful, in honour of You.

Each day
I will grow my heart a little bigger
I will be grateful, in honour of You.

Each day
I will breathe a little deeper
I will be grateful, in honour of You.

Each day

I will release disappointments

I will be grateful, in honour of You.

Each day

I will untie knots of regrets for tomorrow's sake

I will be grateful, in honour of You.

And if I fail

I will try again, each and every new day

I will be grateful, in honour of You.

The Sun cherishes Her Sunflower

Sunflower stands tall, magnificent and bold.

Her perfectly layered honeycomb-yellow ruff exposes an elegant sequence of two thousand florets.
Her yolk-yellow ray florets flap gently in a light breeze.
Her head secure in its receptacle, is laced in delicate green phyllaries.

Sunflower embodies faith, loyalty and adoration.

She basks in the brilliance of her majestic Sun, soaking up sustenance.
She tracks her Sun closely from East to West indulging in Her Goodness.
She is strengthened by the agape bond between her and her Sun.

Sunflower cherishes her Sun.

The Sun and His bride

Sun always radiates love for His bride
His exquisite sun-kissed beauties glow
Secure in the warmth of His affection.

Sunflowers bare vulnerability instead of pride
Embrace His love because they know
He reaches for His bride in reconciliation.

Sunflower reflects Sun

Scintillating Sunflower absorbs Life
And reflects The Source of Life.

Stunning Sunflower is nesting ground
To kaleidoscope of brilliant butterflies.

Sumptuous Sunflower provides greenery
To solitary beaming bees.

Striking Sunflower gives nourishment
To hungry captivating caterpillars.

Splendid Sunflower is goodness

    To birds, bats, bugs,
        racoons, rabbits, rats,
        slugs, squirrels, seed weevils,
        Ladybirds, ladybugs and
        Voles.

Head bowed low, ladened with life
From the scintillating, stunning,
      sumptuous, striking,
      splendid Sunflower
      spread seeds
For the new cycle to begin again.

In life and in death, Sunflower the Sustainer,
emulates the Source of Life.

Sunflower: the proverbial woman

An excellent woman
Capable and intelligent
Of value and is of valour
 Comforter and encourager all the days of her life.

A willing woman
Hunter and gatherer
Ingenious shells for purple
Entrepreneur and visionary all the days of her life.

A compassionate woman
Nurse and nursemaid
Lifts the lowly
Strong and dignified all the days of her life.

A wise woman
Purposeful and motivated
Harnesses potential
Reverent and trusting all the days of her life.

My two joys

Two women of beauty
You may protest 'they are yours'
Shows partisanship not gallantry
Hear me out and you will agree.

These women of tenacity
(Believe me, many a cause for acrimony)
With golden hearts of felicity
Give tiny little gifts of happiness
Wrapped in a smile.
Hearts of service is their style

You be judge and preside
Is this world not a better place for chivalry?
To rescue young and old for a moment or three.

To 3-year-old Hattie

My dear Hattie,

There are many assortments of beautiful peoples, brown, yellow, pale, and fair. And a rainbow of shades in each. People are like distinct types of beautiful flowers and each flower has many assorted colours, all beautiful.

These different beautiful peoples are all one race – the human race. They all share the same pain and joy. They all can learn to love but choose to hate. They all can learn to live in harmony but choose to live in discord. They all can be good custodians of Planet Earth but choose to exploit it.

My dearest Hattie, let it not be so with you. Love all peoples till you burst. Let your love be caught and spread like a virus through the people you meet and passed on. Share your laughter and your joy and let peace reign. Take care of Planet Earth and she will take care of you.

My dear dearest Hattie, stay pure and beautiful. And in ten, twenty, or thirty years, when you read my letter again, let it remind you of the important things that matter in life.

With all my love,

Love.

India

How vibrant are your colours?
Reds, yellows, pinks, greens, and purples.
My! Purple with bright greens and yellows with bright pinks
For spices, saris, and scarves.

How noisy are your streets?
Lorries, tuk tuks, cars and motorbikes.
My! Lorries and cars. Motorbikes and tuk tuks!
For families, favours and fun.

How beautiful are your animals?
Squirrels, monkeys, butterflies, and birds.
My! Red, yellow, and black squirrels, brown monkeys, and bright white birds.
For beauty, bounty, and blessings.

How creative are your peoples?
Artists, sculptors, cooks, and textiles designers
My! Cooks and sculptors, textiles designers and artists.
For sharing, savouring, and serenity.

Say hello to tomorrow

Is everything under the sun meaningless?

A smile.

A look.

A touch.

A gurgle.

A lake.

A mountain.

Is the pursuit of wisdom meaningless?

To grow.

To share.

To keep.

To live.

To venture.

Is the search for labour meaningless?

For birth.

For here.

For now.

For hope.

For tomorrow.

As time goes by

Elusive as time is, it can be trapped in a moment of awe.

Time stands still as I have a bluebell moment.

Time stands still as I walk along the quiet waters.

Time stands still as I listen to the performance of a skylark choir.

Time stands still as I watch a robin flutter and a blue tit dip and skip along in the air.

Time stands still as the juice of a ripe mango trickle down my fingers, forearms, and elbows, as I bite into its succulent flesh.

And at those moments of 'flow', Houdini is captured, and I self-actualise in real Time.

For just one minute

Please stop the clock for just one minute
I want to take in some air and catch my breath.
I need to put my baggage down and soothe the knots in my shoulders.

Please wait patiently for me to join you in the land of the frenetic.
I love the adrenalin shots and the chase of one more victory.
I love to plunder the depths of my ambitions and pillage my youth.

Please Sir, this demands you make, are they really worth it?
Will I enjoy lapping in the fountain of success?
Is my person of such little worth?

Please let me run in the fields of pleasure for its own reward.
I want to lay and just be

I need to kick off my shoes and feel the grass between my toes
And restore rest in my fatigued soul.

Home

Home is where the heart is
And my heart is in picturesque Tewin.
Host to cyclists and walkers.
Residents wave in greeting
And ask after you and yours.

For the sheer joy that is
Village life, welcoming is adorable Tewin.
Quaint fêtes and tweets
Maybe a little gossiping
And yet peaceful and harmonious.

Bury me where my heart is
St Peter's that is, on the hill in beautiful Tewin.
Many wandering years
Monrovia, Accra, Peking, Benin,
Geneva, Belgium to Seaford's shores.

Tewin my home, is where my heart is.

The Journey Motif; River Mimram

Lady Mimram lies sprawled over many miles
A spring at Whitwell to the River Lea.
She meanders through sleepy villages
Resplendent in diamonds that glisten and sparkle in the April sun.

Lady Mimram lends her grace to the swan, to flout its beauty.
Home to tweets, caws, cheeps, chirps, twitters in harmony with the loll, trickle, lapping of the lazy melodic water.

Lady Mimram sustains, nurtures and shelters yet
Exploited, overfished trout, water abstraction, cattle grazing, even milling, says the Domesday Book.

Lady Mimram birthed from a spring, morphs to a river
As is life, from womb to grave.
The grave: a new genesis.

Come let us ponder together

Come sit and ponder with me
Can we take our treasures to the beyond?
No, nothing but treasured souls.

Come let's ponder some more
Can we inherit more than love?
No, nothing but the inherent.

Come ponder and unpeel this word love
Can we earn, make, or formulate this emotion?
No, nothing but luxuriate and bask in it.

Come shall we not ponder our destiny
Can we negotiate or strive for life or death?
No, nothing more ponderous save Love, Life and Death.

LOVE AND DEATH

~0~

Soon, I will lose all three dear brothers

I have seventy years of them in me,

Etched in the fibre of my being.

Laughter and tears.

Laughter, of hills rambled, of stolen cakes scoffed in secret, of holidays by the sea, of setting farts alight and scorched bums!

Tears, for a mother bound by a year-long-prison in her failing body, for a hardworking father cut down in his prime, for wasted time on fruitless pursuits.

 Soon, I will lose all three dear brothers.

I am well acquainted with loss,

Bereft when school took you.

Empty and serene.

Empty, of your mischievousness, of tales of the loves of a teenage man, of the joy of culinary accomplishments.

Serene, for a peace to end the nine-month-pain, for the out-of-control runaway disease called cancer, unbridled by medication.

Soon, I will lose all three dear brothers.

The youngest, vulnerable to taunts.

Troubled by life's injustices.

Vulnerable and belonging.

Vulnerable to the mischievous pranks of an elder brother, to the scares from underneath his bed on dark nights woken by loud playful shouts.

Belonging to our shared history, your voice and mine. Same stories, told in many ways, to our children and their children, my hope and yours belong together.

Soon, I will lose all three dear brothers.

I will attend all three funerals,

Living on borrowed time.

Survivor and guilty.

Survivor of prostate cancer, speeding cars, five daughters and two wives. Of three brothers, two parents, one father-in-law and countless aunts and uncles.

Guilty for holding on to life, for the laughs I will have without you, for the strength I still have, for the joy I will have seeing your grandchildren grow.

Laughter and tears,

Empty and serene,

Vulnerable and belonging,

Survivor and guilty,

Soon, I will lose all three dear brothers.

Addendum

And now the time has come.

To cry

Not for those gone but

For nieces, nephews, sisters-in-law and friends.

Those gone, live on.

Engraved in memory.

Coronavirus

Abruptly, the stealthy killer pounces on unsuspecting victims, holds them captive in feverish paralysis, panting for life.

Its surreptitious seventy-two-hour-long stubborn survival stint camouflages its covert operation. Its only kryptonite, soap and hot water.

Like a leach it grips its host and suffocates, it preys on the weak and the strong, the old and the young, the tough and the vulnerable, a Prime Minister and a bus driver.

Stockpile of corpses in the USA, United Kingdom, Italy, Spain and more besides.

Rows of lonely coffins, friendless, as dispassionate death mediators send them on their way.

Tears yet to be shed for many losses; health, life, freedom, trust, space, and time.

Superheroes called nurses and doctors, ransom its victims with hours of love, with and without protection.

In a moment, many, then a few more, then many more are conquered and silenced across the globe.

Crusaders of engineers launch a pincer movement against the killer, armed with ventilators and respirators. Slowly in the tens, then hundreds and then thousands.

Crusaders of scientists plan a trojan attack, across the globe to disarm the killer, slowly with tests, eventually vaccines. Not one country, nor two, but tens.

Crusaders of champions launch a love campaign to feed the Superheroes, to feed their neighbours, to commune with quidnuncs through the web, to entertain, to endure isolation, slowly one and two messages, then not tens, but hundreds.

The streets fall silent, the hunted in hiding hold their breath, and wait and wait, days turn into weeks, weeks into months surely not many more months….

Frontline daughter

We cried for equality.

We got choice.

My precious out there, exposed.

She dons her alter-ego, puts on her superpower and marches to war.

Fallen heroes about her. She is confident she chose well. Oh, the invincibility of love!

I cry for safety.

I get Terror.

My diamond out there, exposed.

I hold on to Hope, ask my higher power as she marches to war.

Mourners on knees for heroes. They have an aversion for death. Oh, the invincibility of love!

Baby

Mother, dreads her new-born's first greeting from Personally Protected Equipped, Expert Heroes.

Self-sufficient in her cocooned nest, she imagines the peril of a visit to a hothouse of the virus. The life-suckers lurk on gowns, steel equipment, baby units...

Scarce, black market, anti-bacterial cleansers at the ready by the gallons

Mother, diligent from embryo to birth, holds her breath.

Statistics on her side, 'Please, baby be alright'.

Where will the insidious vermin be?

A forgotten speck on which gown or apron?

0.06 microns on the delivery bed?

On the nurse's exposed forearm?

Doctor's stethoscope? Doula's scarf?

Fourteen days later, exhale.

Strange sighting on a Turkish beach

A boy in a red t-shirt, long black shorts and sensible shoes, sighted face down, on the beach.
The World gasped.
Gates slammed: no room in my country for
Cockroaches.
Persecution.
Annihilation.
A generation sentenced to purgatory, refugee camps
Their antagonist disguised as protector.
We turned our backs.

Now, seas of faces, all blurred into one, dressed in hospital gowns, face up in ventilators and respirators.
The World gasps.
Gates ajar: thousands of fallen soldiers
Pandemic.
Apathy.
Anxiety.
A generation sentenced to isolation, fractured clans
The adversary donning invisible camouflage.
We stand to attention.

Goodbye-ing Turk

Thirteen years ago, a dog called Turk was born.
The bouncy Labrador Retriever joined our home.
Grandpa Turk loved Turk.

Soon, it was named 'Disobedient Dog'.
It munched on glasses, shoes and stuffed toys.
It jumped on kitchen counters and sniffed out hidden food.

Disobedient dog, nosed around for food, scraps off the kitchen counter and the dining table. It sat to beg for food with large wet pitiful eyes as it watched each spoonful travel from plate to mouth.

Grandpa Turk melted and always gave in, to that elongated slimy drool and sorrowful sad eyes sorrowful.

Disobedient Dog loved walks. When he glimpsed its lead, it wagged its tail furiously and jumped excitedly.

Every walk was a tug-of-war from start to end.
A tug for every scent that had to be sniffed analytically.
And every other tree had to be marked with a drip.

Disobedient Dog walked into passers-by, sniffed them, in return for a pat on the head. And then happily it would trot off.

Everyone loved Disobedient Dog.
The walkers, the walkers' dogs,
the old ladies on their way to the shop,
those who sat outside the village pub,
the brownies on the green earning their badges,
the boys waiting for a game of football, the old men sat on benches, catching their breath.
The village green was the epicentre for attention.

Suddenly, it was ten. A little bulge appeared on its hind leg.

Disobedient Dog became Disobedient Doggy-Woggy Turk.
The bulge did not cause him trouble
he trotted happily on his walks.
His ears hurt but he loved a rub around his ears.
He chased foxes, squirrels, and cats, not even a limp.

His appetite waned.
One morning, Disobedient Doggy-Woggy Turk ate his breakfast!
The bulge now a tennis ball.
A surprise that was!

Then, no food.
His bowl stood untouched.
Afternoon came and went.
Evening came and went.

Next morning, Disobedient Doggy-Woggy Turk did not eat.
Grandpa Turk paced back and forth and Disobedient Doggy-Woggy was gone.

Thirteen years later, Disobedient Doggy-Woggy Turk died.

The ambling loving Labrador Retriever left our home.

We all loved Disobedient Doggy-Woggy Turk.

I have lost my dog and my father

I had never lived with a dog before I met Turk.
Turk the large, pathetic, black labrador retriever.
I had often stared at the creature and wondered what purpose he served?
Turk, the idle dog with an insatiable appetite.
I hated chewed shoes, broken furniture and soiled carpets.
Turk the untrained, unruly, disobedient dog.

Turk the great listener, his spirited tail wagged furiously, possessed by happiness in response to miniscule attention. Turk, the best walking companion.

The sprightliest of trots wound down to a heavy amble, as the grey hairs sprouted sporadically. His appetite did not wane, till the thirteenth year ended.

Turk now lives in a field smiling on to his walking turf. My father lies achingly facing a brick wall. Now, I shall have to come face to face with my father's sixteen-year end.

The gap in my heart

I would have loved you.
  But you would not let me in.
I hoped for my fair portion of your love, your child.
   But could not earn it.
I hold your life story in my head.
   But my heart has no memory of you.
I let the time roll, and the ache eases.
   But distance slowly fades your face
and leaves behind a gap where you, my father, should be.
You cannot let me in, the grave, a gaping chasm.
Cost far too much
My heart has no muscle memory of the gap that was you
And your outline has faded into yesterday's background

What about me?

Why should I cry for your loss?
You have had seventy years!
I have had thirty.

I will leave behind my baby and my love.

I have tears just for me.
You hid from the storms of your marriage, fled, and abandoned me too!

Our Paradise could not withstand the storms.
My sisters and I scarred by the tsunami of mum's infidelity.
You sailed away in a dinghy of self-protection.

At least you have had seventy years of them in you,
I have ten years of you in me.
I cannot cry for your loss.
You do not cry for mine.

You enjoy the arms of your black whore, her laughter, and her smiles,
As she bleeds you of all that is mine,
Your penance will never be paid.
I hold a grudge and I hold it well.

Dear dad

Dear dad,

I write to you in your grave, two decades have since passed, and a lifetime between.

It is with regret I recognise we parted as strangers.

Twenty long misunderstood years together
Today I glimpse what could have been.

It is with regret I comprehend fatherhood from strangers.

Life is good and I know the greatest Dad of All!

Signing off,
The loved one.

Dear mum is scared to stay with me.

May I ask this question
No response needed.

If mum stayed with me
Fell down the stairs.
Me, away from her, at the top of the stairs
She at the bottom.
Would you believe I had no hand in it?

And if she said I pushed her?

May I ask this question.
No response needed.

If mum stayed with me
Fell down the stairs.
Me close to her, brushed past her
She lost her footing.
Would you believe I had no hand in it?

And if she said I pushed her?

I am scared
If mum stays with me
Warped words would hang me
I would not believe me, if I stood outside
And she fell down the stairs

She would push me. I would have no hand in it.

The cost of food, baby sister

Sis, you have the right to consume
To eat and not think of tomorrow
Who you leave behind by the tightening of your arteries?

Sis, you have the right to negate my plea
Mercy for your girls
Hold on for your offspring's adulthood
A cataclysmic end to the miracle, that is you!

Sis, I oppose your death wish
Leniency is my plea
I fail to love you well
The harder I embrace, the harder you wriggle free.

Sis, see your offspring stranded motherless
Pity, their foreboding desolation
Forsaken on life's barren plain.
The more you consume, the shriller your cry for love.

Sis, hear your heart and blood pressure shriek
'Desist!'
Stretched and worn, faithful to you
Your body yearns the love your heart desires.
The richer your food today, the poorer we will be.

Someone I should know well

She is not dead
Yet she is dead to me

  Enough is never enough
   A deep well of emptiness I cannot fill

     I strive to breathe life into her
     She ambles zombie-like through life
     Shielded by a travesty of laughter

She asks for more
from my empty well

   A full stop enforced
   A concrete defence erected

     I am free of the noose to mend her
     Death to a love that never was
     To a time never had.

Trans: life adrift

You sculpt nature's beauty into your identity from the outside.
Your true identity remains encased in your carcass.

The desecration of nature's beauty will not yield to flagellation to uncover your you.

You sound the same, your animals dance to your love
Yet you search for you.

You have earned a VIP seat in the Trans World
Your people dance to your love
Yet your search for you leads you away from you.

You, Me, or Us

Is marriage a sacrifice of self
Or a preservation of self?

Do you marry a friend and
Or a passionate lover?

Do you shield your heart
Or lay love bare?

Is marriage for sharing
Or clinging on to possessions?

Do you draw up a contract
Or do you trust?

Is marriage designed for all
Or a select few?

The Odyssey of marriage begins with a determined vow.

The value of woman

She is discarded.

Loving mum and dad's unwanted gift lie face buried in mud; lifeless.

Discarded proposal.

Honour says, stuff shame and mummify the living female body for a lifetime of dross.

Exterminated rat,
Disposed.

Pest control

One family, one child
The greater of the two: male.

Unshed cries silenced
Embers of life snuffed

Sent to far off lands. Extinct
HER biography rewritten

Over population, exportation
The greater plight, Choice

A dearth of wives
Lost sisters and daughters.

One family, one nation
The greatest for all: Love.

My son

You are mine.
My flesh.

Let me die before you.
You bury me, not I you.
You are my child!

Why leave me now,
We are too young to die?
And you, younger still.

I place my heart in your coffin.
My flesh
My child.

Shackles

My worth?
Place a sum on me.

Slave to your brutality.
No name, no passport.

My soul?
The price of your soul.

Detached and snubbed out.
No light, no one is home.

My labour?
Spent for my hate of you.

Shackles tightened by the interest
Yet to be paid on my debt.

My life?
Soon to be exterminated.

The cusp of death

Life slowly leaks
Seeps through, seeping, seep, seep, seep.

Soul drains through the pores of life.

In trickles
It drips out, trickling, trickle, trickle, trickle.

Gains momentum, gushes out
A living, breathing embodied entity, shuts down.

Gone.

Printed in Great Britain
by Amazon